D1500189

FEB 2 0

PENNYWISE

Kenny Abdo

Fly!
An Imprint of Abdo Zoom
abdobooks.com

abdobooks.com

Published by Abdo Zoom, a division of ABDO, P.O. Box 398166, Minneapolis, Minnesota 55439. Copyright © 2020 by Abdo Consulting Group, Inc. International copyrights reserved in all countries. No part of this book may be reproduced in any form without written permission from the publisher. Fly!™ is a trademark and logo of Abdo Zoom.

Printed in the United States of America, North Mankato, Minnesota.
052019
092019

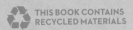
THIS BOOK CONTAINS RECYCLED MATERIALS

Photo Credits: Alamy, Everett Collection, Shutterstock
Production Contributors: Kenny Abdo, Jennie Forsberg, Grace Hansen
Design Contributors: Dorothy Toth, Neil Klinepier

Library of Congress Control Number: 2018963562

Publisher's Cataloging-in-Publication Data

Names: Abdo, Kenny, author.
Title: Pennywise / by Kenny Abdo.
Description: Minneapolis, Minnesota : Abdo Zoom, 2020 | Series: Hollywood monsters set 2 | Includes online resources and index.
Identifiers: ISBN 9781532127496 (lib. bdg.) | ISBN 9781532128479 (ebook) | ISBN 9781532128967 (Read-to-me ebook)
Subjects: LCSH: Clowns--Juvenile literature. | It (Motion picture)--Juvenile literature. | Horror films--Juvenile literature. | Motion picture characters--Juvenile literature.
Classification: DDC 791.43616--dc23

TABLE OF CONTENTS

PENNYWISE

It follows a group of kids who call themselves the Losers Club. When a menacing clown named Pennywise emerges in their small town, they band together to defeat him.

5

From frightening readers on page to terrorizing movie-goers on the **big screen**, Pennywise is a horror **icon**.

ORIGIN

One day while crossing a bridge, author Stephen King thought of the **troll** that lived under the bridge in the "Three Billy Goats Gruff." King imagined an entire town that had a monster living under it.

9

King wanted Pennywise to be a clown because they scare children more than anything else. "They do have that kind of monstrous thing going for them," he explained.

King wanted Pennywise to be everything children fear. In the book, the clown changes from a werewolf to a mummy, to the shark from *Jaws*, and other monsters.

HOLLYWOOD

Pennywise made his **debut** during the mini-series *It* in 1990. Actor Tim Curry donned the make up and jumpsuit. The series was a giant success with more than 30 million viewers.

You'll float

Septer

#ITM

A movie adaptation was made in 2017. Swedish actor Bill Skarsgård played Pennywise. The actor said that he had intense nightmares while filming.

14

The director kept Pennywise away from the other actors for most of the shoot. When it was time to do a scene together, the kids were genuinely scared of him.

Pennywise has a horrifying presence throughout the movie. He only has four minutes of dialog.

It set several box office records. The movie made more than 700 million dollars. It is the highest-grossing horror film of all time.

LEGACY

Pennywise pops up in many other Stephen King novels. He is mentioned or appears in *The Tommyknockers*, *Dreamcatcher*, and more.

Pennywise is thought to be the inspiration for real-life scary clown sightings. People from across the United States, and even England, have encountered a scary clown similar to Pennywise at night.

The 2019 *It* **sequel** continues the story 27 years later. The adult versions of the Losers Club members are played by Jessica Chastain, James McAvoy, and Bill Hader.

GLOSSARY

big screen – another name for the movies.

debut – a first appearance.

dialog – conversation between two or more people in a book or movie.

gross – to make a profit.

icon – a symbol that represents a certain function or purpose.

sequel – a movie, or other work that continues the story begun in a preceding one.

troll – a mythical monster in folklore that is usually very ugly.

ONLINE RESOURCES

Booklinks
NONFICTION NETWORK
FREE! ONLINE NONFICTION RESOURCES

To learn more about
Pennywise, please visit
abdobooklinks.com or scan
this QR code. These links
are routinely monitored and
updated to provide the most
current information available.

INDEX